# COUNCIL OF SHAHAPIVAN

*444 AD*

St. Hovsep,
*Catholicos of Armenia*

Translated by: D.P. Curtin

Dalcassian
Publishing
Company

# COUNCIL OF SHAHAPIVAN

Copyright @ 2021 Dalcassian Publishing Company

All rights reserved. No part of this publication may be reproduced, distributed, or transmitted in any form or by any means, including photocopying, recording, or other electronic or mechanical methods, without the prior written permission of the publisher, except in the case of brief quotations embodied in critical reviews and certain other non-commercial uses permitted by copyright law. For permission request, write to Dalcassian Publishing Company at dalcassianpublishing at gmail.com

ISBN: 979-8-8691-7258-7 (Paperback)

Library of Congress Control Number:
Author: Curtin, D.P. (1985-)

Printed by Ingram Content Group, 1 Ingram Blvd, La Vergne, Tennessee

First printing edition 2021.

# COUNCIL OF SHAHAPIVAN

# SHAHAPIVAN CANONS (444 AD)

*20 CHAPTERS*

These canons were established by a council of Armenian elders in the seventh year after the death of St. Sahak.

## INSTITUTIONS AND CANONS OF THE HOLY CHURCH, ADOPTED BY THE ARMENIAN VARDAPETS IN ADDITION AND CONFIRMATION OF THE APOSTOLIC AND NICAEAN CANONS

The helmsman must take care of the serviceability of the vessel, notice the paths of the sea and, using the fair wind, sail along the waves of the sea. Likewise, the commander (must) always lead into battle an army of selected men and cavalrymen, armed with weapons, equipped with horses and, trusting only in the battle, so that they might emerge victorious and receive a crown and glory from the king. All the more necessary, should the Vardapets, the shepherds of the Holy Church, the leaders of the laws of justice and the immutable commandments of the living God, always reflect, day and night, on the laws of the Lord and constantly adorn the youths of the Church in the Lord.

After the death of the righteous Vardapet, fathers and true leaders-legislators, especially after the death of the holy high priest Sahak, the Armenian Catholicos and spirit-filled lover of truth, Vardapet Mesrop, who enlightened the Armenian country with his preaching. After their death, there was a distortion and disintegration of the orders and laws of the holy church, as the holy high priest of God Sahak, or even earlier, St. Gregory (the Illuminator), had previously seen in his Vision. Those mired in vile deeds and disgusting morals have multiplied. From the cooling of love, lawlessness multiplied and there was no one to pluck the tares and remove the harmful dodder, for the wheatgrass took root and spread day-by-day. And in the Armenian country, in the house of Torgom, there was an increase of Messalians and other wicked people. Those who leave their wives, harlots, thieves, unauthorized people, and all sorts of evildoers and seducers. And sorrow and sadness came. And those who were previously zealous vardapets, bishops, priests who took a vow of holiness, servants of Christ and children of the holy church, as well as those who belonged to the priestly order, did not follow the righteous path of holiness. And, mainly, because power and dominion at that time were not in the hands of the house of Mamikonyan, for they took refuge and were conquered and subjugated by the ascendant Persian kingdom. Vardan Mamikonyan, and his relatives, together with his brothers, although they grieved, moaned and growled like lion cubs, they were locked as if in a cage and hoped only for help from above. For the malicious Persian nation, suspected and feared them, as did not hand over power to them.

And day-by-day the plan ripened and the night showed the night the unhindered nature of affairs. The news kept pace with itself, and word was passed from person to person. According to a unanimous order, they gathered to the designated place - Shahapivan, to the camp of the Armenian kings, in time for the New Year holiday. And this took place in the sixth year of the reign of the Persian king Yezdegerd and the marzpanism of Vasak Syuni in Armenia and the azarpetism of Vahan Amatuni and the Malkhazism of Vriv Horkhoruni.

And forty bishops and many priests and deacons, zealous ministers, and the entire congregation of the holy church, all the iskhans gathered: regional rulers, regional leaders, supreme judges, treasurers, military leaders, thousands, leaders of localities, Azates from various regions. The senior nakharars of the Armenian country, who were zealous defenders of laws and holiness, unanimously said this: "Restore the order established by Saint Gregory, Nerses, Sahak and Mashtots, and also, according to your will, establish other benefits and we will voluntarily and willingly accept. For the order of the church weakened and people returned to lawlessness. You will establish laws pleasing to God and necessary for the building of his church, and we will obey and strictly observe them. And if anyone does not strictly observe the established laws, be he a bishop, or a priest, or an azat, or a shinakan, let him be punished and pay a fine." And it was unanimously said by the high priests that "The Apostolic and Nicene canons are unshakable and we submit," but with the addition to these canons of what is necessary especially for the house of Torgom and the eastern regions.

# COUNCIL OF SHAHAPIVAN

**Henceforth it was established and established as follows:**

I. If a bishop is convicted of defilement, or fornication, or any other bad deed, and thereby humiliates the apostolic honor and the holy throne, Scripture says about this: "you associate with thieves and associate with adulterers", and if this is established by testimony, excommunicate him from the throne and power and removed from the priesthood, fined 1200 drams in favor of the church and he will be accused: "For he is a man who is in honor and foolish" and distribute the fine to the poor for he must "meditate on the law of the Lord every day and night" and "keep his covenants" and not go astray, but "follow the royal road, not deviate either to the right or to the left," so that the disciples would not accept the same bad teaching.

II. If the priest is in defilement or fornication or in other bad deeds and these deeds are revealed by testimony, remove him from the priesthood, fine him 300 drams and distribute it to the poor and leave him in the rank of readers. And if even in the position of a reader he indulges in the same filth, deprive him of the rank and position of a reader until he is corrected by repentance, and the bishop, seeing his correction, can again introduce him into the ranks of readers for the church needs a saint, especially since the Lord the altar of the sacrament receives the blameless, so as not to awaken the wrath of God on earth through the leaders. If a married priest is convicted of defilement and fornication or other evil deeds and this is proven by witnesses, he will be deprived of the priestly rank and taken away from the church share, fined 200 drams to be distributed to the poor. This canon applies to both the priest and the deacon. And they in the church should stand with the soldiers, be among the taxpayers and not mix with the clergy.
And if the wife of a priest or deacon is convicted of fornication, then let them choose - either the church and the priesthood or a wife. If they choose the priesthood, then the wife must be removed from the house, and strict repentance must be imposed on them. And if the priest's daughter is caught in fornication, deprive her of her share of the church, remove her from the priest's house, and impose strict repentance and punishment. The priest's son should be given the same punishment.

And if a priest dies, his wife should not marry, and also the priest after the death of his wife should not marry. And there should be no harlot servant in the priest's house, "for it is holy to the Lord."

III. If someone has a wife and commits adultery and does not keep holy the vow of marriage and the crown that he received on his head from the holy church through the priest, and the helper that fell to his lot, as it is written about this, that the Lord gave to the husband in his wife's assistants; The Apostle Paul speaks about this: "Let marriage for all be honorable and the bed undefiled," when they are married chastely, "but God will judge fornicators and adulterers." And again: "The wife has no power over her body, but the husband does; Likewise, the husband has no power over his body, but the wife."

So, if someone has trampled on the blessed life and pleasure received from the holy church for the glorification of the Lord, and has desecrated the blessed marriage given by God, given himself over to fornication and adultery and drunkenness, the elders must correct such a person with flogging and edifying speeches, and, excommunicating him from the church], fine for the benefit of the church and distribute to the poor (for the fact that he defamed the church and desecrated the crown of blessing). If he is an azat and is not subject to flogging, increase the fine and penance - 200 drams in favor of the poor, two years of penance and do not repeat the desecration; only after this can he be allowed into the church and into communication with his comrades. If he is a shinakan, flog him thoroughly, fine him 100 drams in favor of the church and distribute it to the poor; a year after he has moved away from defilement, allow him into the church and into communication with his comrades. This canon applies to both husband and wife.

If anyone before marriage was in fornication, whether with a stranger or with his betrothed, a fine for dishonor must be collected, as much as the father and mother of the girl demand as Moses commanded in the laws. If he wishes to take the same girl as his wife, first both must purify themselves by repentance, and if they get married, then they should be married not as virgins, but as bigamous, only by rebaptism.

And if fornication took place at the will of the girl, then the father and mother of the girl should not be fined, but a fine of 100 drams should be collected from the man and 50 drams from the girl in favor of the church and distributed to the poor.

If one of them is a virgin, and the other has committed fornication, bless the virgin as a virgin, and place a cross-shaped willow on the head of the fornicator as a bigamist, as a sign of victory over the enemy, and continue to be careful.

IV. If a husband leaves his wife, the mother of children, not as a result of her adultery or any bad bodily vice, but because of his fornication and infatuation with another woman, then the court will be as follows: divide equally the children and the house, property and land, water and in general, give everything, half to the wife, and also, if she wishes, give her the right to freely bring another husband into her house. Let everyone take his share and pay the entire government taxes. And impose on the husband who abandoned his wife a seven-year penance and a fine in favor of the church, if he is an Azat, in the amount of 300 drams; if he is a shinakan, flog him and fine him in favor of the church in the amount of 100 drams for neglecting the blessed marriage.

If any woman dares, even before the end of the year, to marry someone who has abandoned his wife while he is in discord and under fine, and it becomes clear that she was the reason for the husband's abandonment of his first wife, then this woman should be detained and handed over to a leper colony, where she must grind grain for lepers for one year. If she is from Azat and does not go to the leper colony, collect from her a fine of 100 drams in favor of the lepers.

V. If someone takes a wife who turns out to be barren and leaves her because of barrenness, then she has the right to take the property she brought into the house of her husband - servants, cattle, clothes, silver - and leave. And if she has no vice, other than infertility, her husband must also pay her a fine for insult in the amount of 1,200 drams if he is an azat, and 600 drams if he is a shinakan.
If during the time he is on trial and under a fine, and before the expiration of one year, any woman dares to marry him, then this woman should be detained and sent to a leper colony, for it is clear that she was the reason for the husband's abandonment of his wife. Such a woman must grind grain for lepers for a year and serve in a leper colony, and also pay a fine of 100 drams to the church for causing the dissolution of a valid marriage. If she is from Azat and does not go to the leper colony, then let her pay a fine of 100 drams in favor of the lepers.
But if the husband promised her in advance to leave his wife and take her, or was burning with adulterous love for her, then he is subject to a fine in favor of the church in the amount of 100 drams and penance: for three years he must remain

among the listeners and only after a year, after that may be admitted to the church.

Anyone who leaves his wife - the mother of children or barren without the fact of adultery or other vice, in relation to him, as well as the woman who married him, let the punishment, fine and penance provided for by this canon and regulation be in force.

VI. If a wife leaves her husband, let them detain her and return her to her husband again, especially if she married for a ransom, and not as a harlot; Even if she sold herself and hired herself as a servant, then her husband, if he wishes, let him keep her with spiritual and good instruction and with love.

If the husband himself is malicious or a fornicator or a carouser and a drunkard, or suffers from some other vice, then let them teach him a lesson with flogging and instruction and reconcile them. If he is from the Azats, then let them call him to order with a fine and instruction. If the husband quickly corrects himself, then the wife should honor him.

VII. If a girl is kidnapped, then let her be found and returned to her father and mother; from the kidnapper, if he is an azat, a fine in favor of the parents in the amount of 1200 drams should be collected for insult, but if he is a shinakan - 600 drams. And the assistants of the false bridegroom, participants in the raid, should be fined each in the amount of 100 drams, with half of the fine deducted in favor of the church and half in favor of the poor. If the false groom committed fornication with a girl without a wedding, collect from him a fine of 100 drams in favor of the church and subject him to penance for three years for insulting the crown of blessing. The priest who married them secretly, without the knowledge of the girl's father and mother, will be deprived of his priestly rank and fined 100 drams in favor of the poor; the wedding is declared invalid. If, after this outrage and fine, the girl, as well as her father and mother, still agree to marry the kidnapper, then if they had previously committed fornication, the wedding ceremony cannot be performed on them; in this case, a cross-shaped willow is placed on them, as on bigamous people. If they remain virgins, then their marriage is blessed by law. This canon applies equally to both azat and shinakan.

VIII. If anyone, man or woman, is convicted of witchcraft, apostasy or other atrocity, and does not regret and repent, he, according to the commandment of Scripture, is subject to stoning. If they repent, they are subject to penance for life: they must remain at the threshold of the church with the listeners for twelve years, and then only they can be admitted to the church, and there they must spend three years with the penitents; and they must constantly help the poor with alms and mercy, distributing to the poor a lot of property for the salvation of their souls, and by diligent repentance they will be worthy of communion before death.

IX. Whoever turns to fortune tellers or sorcerers is subject to a fine of 200 drams in favor of the poor, if he is an azat; if he is a shinakan, subject him to 15 blows, and also fine him 100 drams in favor of the poor; after a three-year penance they can receive communion.

And if a bishop or priest turns to the soothsayers, and this is confirmed by the testimony of two or three witnesses, for it is written: "Accept an accusation against a presbyter only in the presence of two or three witnesses", the bishop should be deprived of his episcopal rank and the priest of his priestly rank; fine the bishop 1000 drams, and the priest 500 and distribute it to the poor in the church, and they will be accused, for: "Is there no God in Israel, that you go to ask Beelzebub, the deity of Ekron?".

And if one of the clergy and hieromonks, or the son of a priest, joins the soothsayers, then they are subject to punishment, fines, penances established for the laity, and deprivation of the rank of clergy. This canon applies equally to both men and women who turn to fortune tellers.

X. About those who only cast magic, but do not cast spells. If a man or woman is caught in witchcraft, they should be given 15 double blows, branded, covered with soot, their bones dislocated, and given to a leper colony, where they must grind for lepers for two years and do whatever they are ordered to do. If the guilty Azat does not go to the leper colony, collect from him a fine of 500 drams in favor of lepers, and for another two years he must repent in his church and then take communion and not sin again.

XI. Who will cry over the dead man and mourn him in despair, forgetting farewell with hope and blessing about which the sermon speaks: "And if in this life alone we hope in Christ, then we are the most miserable of all people," and "so that you do not grieve for the dead , like others who have no hope", so, if one of the Azats or Shinakans opposes the apostolic canon and mourns the deceased, let the mourner and the one crying be cursed. For a year they must not enter the church and must also pay a fine: azat - 100 drams and shinakan - 50 drams for the benefit of the poor, for by their behavior they angered God and disturbed the souls of the dead, God will be reconciled through offerings to the poor; and the deceased will have peace. And in particular, if the dying person did not order to mourn, and the family mourned, as was said, then those who mourn and cry will be deprived of blessings and removed from the church. And the family cannot serve the liturgy over the deceased, because they are subject to penance. But for the sake of the deceased, priests and ministers must serve mass on their own behalf, as he deserves, until the family returns to order and remembers the name in the holy sacrament, so that souls may rest in peace. But if the deceased ordered to mourn him during his lifetime, then the fine established by the canons is paid in double amount, and the family and mourners are subject to the established punishment, and no one should serve the liturgy for the deceased, and nothing should be done in his memory and his name should not be remembered because of his hopelessness.

XII. If a son has his father's wife instead of a wife, about which Paul, turning to the Corinthians, always shouted and screamed that: "And it also happened that a man has his father's wife instead of a wife" and said: "You must be cut off and taken out of your midst whoever did such a deed and deliver it over to Satan, so that the spirit may be saved on the day of the Lord." So, for example, Reuben the son of Jacob was cursed because he slept with his father's concubine. So, if someone has his father's wife instead of a wife, the canon does not recognize him, he must not enter the holy church, and let him be cursed by all believers until he comes to his senses, serves seven years of repentance in the audience and three years with the penitent, and pays a fine - 50 drams in favor of the poor, 50 drams in favor of the church, and only after his lifestyle has been checked can he be allowed to receive communion.

If a father has his son's wife instead of a wife, or a brother has his brother's wife, let there be the same punishments and curses. Let no one dare to marry a close relative or relative or commit adultery with her.

And if cohabitation took place at the will of the woman, let her be given the same punishments, fine and curse, impose penance and send her to a leper colony, where she will have to grind grain for lepers for ten years. If she is from Azat and will not go to the lepers, then let her give 300 drams in favor of the lepers.

XIII. No one should take a relative as his wife. Let this defilement and abomination not be known and not be listed among you, for no one should mix the dirt of his belly, according to the custom of pagans and ungodly peoples, as the great Lawgiver, the prophet Moses, received a command from the Creator about this: "Declare to the children of Israel that no one should approach any blood relative, announce this to them in parables." And Moses wrote a curse, cursed be the one who sleeps with a blood relative. So, whoever is devout remains in Christianity and in the baptism of the Lord - bears the seal and sign of the king of heaven, is not free to marry his sister, or his mother's brother's daughter, or his brother's daughter, or his father's sister, or another woman from his family up to the fourth generation so that there is no distortion of the holy faith, for such a one "stores up wrath for himself." "The children of adulterers will be imperfect, and the seed of the wicked bed will disappear." And if the head of the great prophet and forerunner John, who reproached Herod, only because he took possession of his brother's wife was cut off, then should not it be considered a greater misfortune if someone takes a relative by blood as his wife, which is prohibited by Christian laws, the holy apostles and disciples of Christ. So, if anyone resists the laws and the canon now established and becomes an ungodly pagan and Jew, he will perish; his share will be with him and let him be alienated from the holy church, as it is written: "Let the wicked disappear from the earth and not look at the greatness of the Lord," "and be counted among the evildoers," as it is written: "Depart from me, all who do lawlessness," let no one accept his sacrifice, for his sacrifice is unclean before the Lord. If the offerer is filthy, then how much more filthy is his sacrifice. The Church and the canons do not accept his repentance, for "What is corrupt will be removed from me; I will not know evil," until they leave and turn away from their depravity and evil deeds, according to the word of the prophet: "Stop doing evil, says the Lord".

If anyone blesses the marriage of such people or goes to the wedding, he will be an accomplice in evil deeds and should be removed from service. And if a bishop or priest turns out to be involved, then they should be deprived of the throne and the priesthood and not allowed to perform the service. But if those who have deviated from the laws of the saints and the order of the church turn away from an unclean marriage and get divorced, then they will make great sacrifices - giving half of their lives and property in favor of the poor unfortunates and the holy church, spending their lives in repentance, at death only may receive communion.

And also, the leaders of the church involved in this, and the one who blessed the crown, must pay a fine in favor of the poor - the bishop 500 drams, the priest 200 drams, as well as the one who blessed the crown 200 drams, and then only they can be admitted to the throne and priesthood.

If those who entered into an unclean marriage do not divorce, then the crown-bearer and the priests involved in this should not be allowed near the throne or the priesthood; this law and canons are valid for both azat and shinakan.

If anyone, speaking out against it, says why the Nicene canons do not provide for such severe punishments, then you should know that then no one could have foreseen how many evils and crimes would be committed in the world, otherwise the evil would have been eradicated without delay.

XIV. A bishop or priest or deacon, or any of the clergy, or from the congregation should not keep a housekeeper, as is customary among the Messalians. If anyone holds, and this is established by testimony, he will be deprived of his dignity, no matter what he may be, and he will be considered as a wicked publican, for the holy church and the holy sacrament of the Lord accepts the blameless, for the vicious must be saved blameless.

XV. If anyone remains in the faith or wants to be a hermit, preserve virginity and holiness and achieve eternal life, let him live with fellow truthful and hermits, and let them benefit each other with the love of Christ, for "A brother who helps a brother is like a fortress wall," and also "God brings the lonely into the house," and "for where two or three are gathered in My name, there am I in the midst of them"; and again: "If two people in agreement ask from my Father, it will be done for them"; "By this everyone will know that you are my disciples, if you have love for one another." It is impossible for only custom to exist, let alone how people could know the position and conditions of faith, or be aware of their crimes, or show their humility and love for their comrades. Such are the animals in the mountains, which remain peacefully until no one approaches them. But perfect and true faith consists of the following: humility towards loved ones and love for each other and for Christ, to be a good example and prototype among people in order to benefit each other and to be zealous in good deeds. (So that they may see and bless the Lord in heaven). And the one who brings a dishonest brother who has stumbled through spiritual edification into the number of worthy ones will be called by the mouth of God. But come, my sons, and listen, and let the fear of the Lord be your teacher to eternal life, and during your lifetime you will see the warning of days of kindness; listen and learn what pleases the Lord and encourages you to eternal life. Keep your tongue from evil and deceit. Know that an evil tongue is a fire contained in the body; smooth out the wrinkles of injustice; Close the doors of your lips tightly - the protection of your lips, and do not lean towards evil deeds. Don't give silver at interest and don't take interest as surplus. Soon returning the debtor's pledge. Sons of men, how long will you be hard-hearted, impatient without cause? Who can restrain an impatient person? From bloodshed, strangulation, adultery, fornication, theft, greed, love of money, false oaths, lies, tricks, drunkenness, gluttony, arrogance, stubbornness, conceit, arrogance. Do not be a proud ill-wisher, arrogant; do not participate in round dance games, in the songs of insolent people, do not dress up, do not mock in vain, do not riot; do not oppress, do not grumble, do not be hateful, impudent, talkative, do not speak or listen to gossip about anyone, and what seems evil to you, do not do to another; do not be lustful, sleepy, stubborn in your studies, so as not to indulge in evil, do not be lazy in prayers, do not hate the poor, so that on a bad day they will save you and not betray you into the hands of the enemy; do not hate fasting and asceticism, which extinguish fire, tame lions and fulfill the word addressed to God, as well as other good deeds are carried out completely, with love from the bottom of your heart for the Lord God and the fulfillment of his commandments. One should live in peace with all people, be meek and humble, and be in awe and fear every hour and listen to his words, which read: "On whom I will look, but one who is humble and contrite in spirit and who trembles at my word"; "Seek peace and follow truth." One should hope with hope, not grieve and be sad for nothing, "and not lose heart in doing good." For ever and ever a perfect man will live in heaven and appear as an angel on earth. Anyone who wants to be a hermit and immaculate and accept monasticism must adhere to this canon in order to remain in the faith, for with the help of the immaculate sinners will be cleansed.

XVI. Whoever wants to be a bishop, leader and shepherd, or a monk, or wants to build a monastery, and wants leadership over a district, or villages and monasteries, let him listen to what they say: "When wealth increases, do not put your heart on it." Anyone who borrows money should be on guard; they may demand it back with interest; Be careful, shepherd of the flock, be prepared!
No one should become a bishop without the will of the chief bishop of the country, and no one without the bishop of the district is free to become an archimandrite of a monastery or a hermit.

If a bishop, or a priest, or a judge from the Azats or Shinakans wants to appoint leaders, prepare pastors of the church and establish leaders and establish legislators: "Let the nations know that they are men," and therefore they take bribes or show partiality and choose not the truth and the worthy, and rich, even if he is one of the most dishonest and despicable: but one should choose only zealots of holiness and laws.

Listen to what they say: "God has chosen the base things of the world and the base things and the base things," and "They raise the poor out of the dirt, seating them with the great, so that the proud and the mighty may be ashamed," "For man looks on the outward appearance, but the Lord looks on the heart." "And they, by bribes and partiality, choose those dishonored by crimes and defiled in faith, as Paul says, as judges of the church for the sake of destructive silver. Let those who give bribes be cursed, like the crucifiers who bribed the guards, and like Simon the Magus, who wanted to receive the grace of the Holy Spirit from the apostles with silver and property. And let those who take bribes be cursed by God. Let the property that they took be considered a bribe from Judas, which he received for betraying the Lord, and let it be returned twice as much. But those who gave a bribe, like the crucifiers who bought land, do not dare take it, but let them distribute it to the needy. And the bishop or priest who will take bribes or anything from property for such deeds, according to the scripture, "For gifts blind the hearts of rulers," and also: "Do not accept gifts against the innocent," and "truth is dragged behind silver," let them be they are cursed by all councils and removed from power and the priesthood. Let a bribe be considered stolen by Geez the leper; let the curse of the prophet fall on him, for the blood of the mighty is required for the innocent. And the worthy ones, after searching, will be found. Listen to the prophet: "Whose hands are wicked and whose right hand is full of bribery." Grant them, Lord, for their deeds of iniquity.

If the base and top are strong, then the middle part is not on sand.

If the driver is drunk, then how will the chariot move?

If the helmsman is asleep, the ship will soon get into trouble.

If the shepherd is slow, then the flock will eat harmful grass, for if the leaders of the law are steadfast and truthful, then all the more will those under them not stumble.

And if the foundation is immovable, then the structure will not be overthrown by the river.

If the shepherd is brave, then the flock will not be eaten by wild animals; if the guard is prudent and vigilant, then the army will be at peace and will not be cut down.

For you, Vardapets, guardians of the people, are an example to the world; looking at you, they appeal to your teaching. So be discerning.

XVII. If anyone wants to install the relics of martyrs, then he should not install them without the permission of the bishop of the country. Without the permission of the bishop, let no one dare to commemorate the martyrs and convene councils. And if anyone from the holy places brings the relics of the martyrs, let him bring them to the bishop with testimonies and papers of those bishops from where he brought them, and, at the order of his bishop, install them where it is worthy.

If anyone wishes to erect an altar to the sacrament of the Lord, then he should not dare to erect it without the permission of the bishop. But in the name of the relics brought, let them annually hold large celebrations on the day of the offering, and one should be careful in honoring and venerating in order to avoid the wrath of the holy hermits who went to martyrdom for Christ, for the country will receive wrath in return for intercession.

XVIII. If a Vardapet cursed, excommunicated or anathematized someone with his Vardapet word: a student, a secular person or a priest, then the Vardapet or a bishop or priest of other localities does not have the right to bless the damned or lift the anathema, unless he corrects himself through faith and spiritual love; after which the peace-loving vardapet will intercede with good edifications so that he submits to his vardapet, for: "One Lord, one faith, one baptism," one commandment for all and one hope; in all churches the same agreement should be maintained: those worthy of blessing should be unanimously blessed and punished. For from universal unanimity the teaching will be stable and true for everyone, according to the word of the Lord: "By this everyone will know that you are My disciples, if you have love for one another."

XIX. If any of the priests or deacons or monks is convicted of messalianism, he will be deprived of the priesthood, have a fox brand burned on his forehead and be sent to repentance to where the hermits live. But if he is caught in this again, then let them cut both veins and give him to the leper colony, for he is "a man who was in honor but did not understand." The monk is also subject to this punishment.

And if people with wives and children are caught in this heresy, then let them cut the veins of men and women and mature children, burn a fox brand on their foreheads and give them to the leper colony for repentance. And children who have not yet known defilement should be selected and handed over to the holy servants of the Lord, so that they can raise and teach them in the true faith and in the fear of God.

XX. If a criminal Messalian is found among the parishioners, and the priests, knowing about this, do not inform the bishop, then when they investigate and find that it is true, and the priest, knowing about their affairs in advance, did not complain to the bishop, then those criminals must bear the punishment established by the canons for the Messalians, and priests should not be allowed to enter the priesthood until the end of their lives, lest another priest or monk take their place. place, looking at them, regularly looked after the parishioners.

If the priest informs the bishop and proves this with testimony, and the bishop, having received a bribe, hides it or becomes partial, then when it is revealed that the priests' complaint actually reached him and he neglected the commandments of God and did not seek out the perishing and did not become a zealot for the laws God and an avenger, in which case he must be dethroned; the priest should be considered innocent.

If the bishop showed diligence and took revenge, and the priests and other persons prove that the bishop showed zeal and handed over the criminal to the authorities, and the ruler, be he the master of the country, or the headman of a village, nakharar - the master of the region, will shield the filth, hide and harbor fornicators, either because of disastrous silver, or partiality and dependence, and does not prefer love for Christ and his commandments and be an avenger for the laws of the Lord, for soul and body, let him be cursed and excommunicated from the holy church until he delivers the libertines into the hands of the bishop.
If in the house of a nakharar, or in his wife, or in his daughter, or in his son, or in himself, filth is discovered, and he does not hand over his family to the bishops and does not himself return to holiness, desiring to be self-governing, then let him be damned with all your home, children and property. Let him not dare to appear among the people, let friends and the world not communicate with him while he is in defilement and until he returns to holiness. If he himself is not in desecration, let him hand over his family and servants to the chief bishop for reproach.

If, as was said, defilement is discovered in the house of the Vostikan, or in himself, or in the family, let them punish the family according to the punishment established by law. If he and his family are convicted of messalianism, let them seize him together with his depraved family, and let them appear publicly before the chief bishop, before the great princes and senior judges, and let them unanimously punish for violating God's laws, so that others, seeing this, sacredly and in fear they honored the Creator of all.

So that through the revenge of the laws and the veneration of the saints we remain healthy and unharmed, so that in word and deed.

The Scriptorium Project is the work of a small group of lay people of various apostolic churches who are interested in the preservation, transmission, and translation of the works of the early and medieval church. Our efforts are to make the works of the church fathers accessible to anyone who might have an interest in Christian antiquities and the theological, philosophical, and moral writings that have become the bedrock of Western Civilization.

To-date, our releases have pulled from the Greek, Syriac, Georgian, Latin, Celtic, Ethiopian, and Coptic traditions of Christianity, and have been pulled from sundry local traditions and languages.

## Other Selections from the Armenian Church Series:

*Refutations* by Eznik of Kolb (Dec. 2007)

*Explanation of the Faith of the Armenian Church* by Nerses IV the Gracious, Catholicos of Armenia (July 2009)

*Super Quibusdam* by Pope Clement VI (Nov. 2009)

*The Life of Mashtots* by Koriun the Iberian (Nov. 2012)

*Letter to Kiwron, Catholicos of Iberia* by Movses II, Catholic of Armenia (Nov. 2013)

*Canons of the Synod of Partav* by Sion I, Catholicos of Armenia (Dec. 2013)

*The History of the Holy Cross of Aparank* by St. Gregory of Narek (Feb. 2014)

*Armenian Synaxarium: Volume I- Month of Navasard* (Oct. 2018)

*The Geography* by Ananias of Shirak (Dec. 2020)

Cum Dudum: a letter to the Armenians by Pope Benedict XII (Nov. 2021)

*Council of Shahapivan (444 AD)* by St. Hovsep, Catholicos of Armenia (Dec. 2021)

*Genealogy of the Family of St. Gregory* by St. Mesrop Mashtots (Nov. 2023)

www.ingramcontent.com/pod-product-compliance
Lightning Source LLC
LaVergne TN
LVHW051924060526
838201LV00060B/4164